Melanin Magic

Affirming Poems for Young Black Hearts

Zakara Jeña

Copyright © 2024 Zakara Jeña
All rights reserved
First Edition

PAGE PUBLISHING
Conneaut Lake, PA

First originally published by Page Publishing 2024

ISBN 979-8-89157-644-5 (pbk)
ISBN 979-8-89157-658-2 (digital)

Printed in the United States of America

To my mom, you have been my greatest inspiration and unwavering supporter throughout my journey. Your love, guidance, and belief in me have propelled me forward, even in the face of challenges. You have instilled in me the values of perseverance, resilience, and the importance of embracing my heritage. Your unwavering support has allowed me to pursue my dreams and become the person I am today. Your encouragement has given me the strength to create this book, empowering young African American children to believe in themselves and unlock their potential. Thank you for being my rock, my confidante, and my guiding light. This book is a testament to the love and inspiration you have showered upon me. I dedicate this work to you, Mom, with deep gratitude and endless love. With all my heart, Zakara Jeña.

My Beautiful Hair

My hair is curly, kinky, and free
It's a part of me, just like my skin, you see
It's thick and strong, it stands up tall
It's my crown, my glory, my all in all
My hair is magic, it can do anything
It can twist, it can turn, it can even sing
It can be braided, it can be styled
It's versatile, it's wild, it's my pride
My hair is unique, it's one of a kind
It's different, it's special, it's mine to find
It's beautiful, it's worthy, it's loved by me
My hair is perfect, just the way it should be
So let's celebrate our hair, let's shout it loud
Let's be proud of our roots, let's wear our crown
Let's embrace our curls, let's show them off
My hair is beautiful, and that's a fact.

Unleashing Possibilities

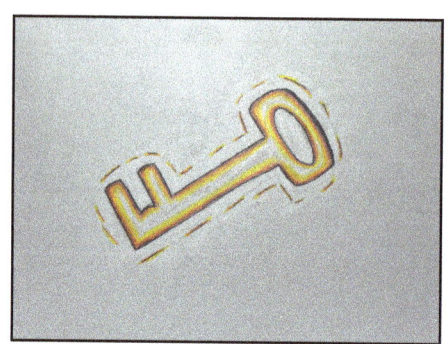

I hold the power to shape my destiny
Dreaming big, achieving what I believe
Reaching for stars, touching skies so high
I'm the one who dares to soar, reaching the sky

A doctor, a teacher, a lawyer, and more
An artist, a writer, an explorer to the core
An athlete, a scientist, a musician in tune
Endless possibilities, my heart's in bloom

Challenges may come, but I won't be deterred
With resilience and hard work, I'll be undisturbed
Learning, growing, reaching for success
I can do anything, I'll overcome any test

So let's believe in ourselves, let faith ignite
Chasing dreams, finding our place, shining bright
Confident and strong, we'll stand tall
In a world of endless possibilities, we'll conquer all!

Zakara Jeña

My Beautiful Skin

My skin is brown, it's rich, it's bold
It's a part of me, it's what I hold
It's smooth and soft, it's strong and true
It's beautiful, it's perfect, it's me, it's you
My skin is magic, it can shine so bright
It can glow, it can radiate, it's a sight
It can be kissed by the sun, it can feel the breeze
It's amazing, it's wonderful, it's here to please
My skin is unique, it's one of a kind
It's a masterpiece, it's what's inside
It tells a story, it holds a history
It's a symbol of strength, it's a victory
My skin is my pride, it's my heritage
It's a symbol of love, it's a message
It's a celebration, it's a work of art
My skin is beautiful, it's a brand-new start.
So let's celebrate our skin, let's shout it loud
Let's be proud of who we are, let's stand out
Let's embrace our beauty, let's show it off
My skin is beautiful, and that's enough.

My Family and Me

My family is my world, it's my heart
It's where I belong, it's where I start
It's a bond that's unbreakable, it's a love that's true
It's a feeling that's indescribable, it's me and you
My family is my support, it's my guide
It's a place where I can be myself, it's where I can hide
It's a shoulder to cry on, it's a hand to hold
It's a warm embrace, it's a heart of gold
My family is my joy, it's my laughter
It's a place where memories are made, it's a happily ever after
It's a place where I'm loved, it's a place to grow
It's a place where I'm happy, it's a place to show
My family is my unity, it's my strength
It's a place where we stand together, it's a journey that's long
It's a place where we support each other, it's a place where we belong
My family is my everything, it's where I belong.
So let's celebrate our family, let's shout it loud
Let's be proud of who we are, let's stand out
Let's embrace our love, let's show it off
My family is beautiful, and that's enough.

The Magic of Kindness

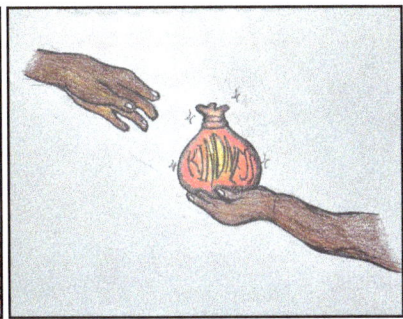

Kindness is a magic, it's a power that's real
It's a gift that keeps giving, it's a way to heal
It's a smile, it's a hug, it's a listening ear
It's a gesture of love, it's a way to show you care
Kindness is a light, it's a beacon of hope
It's a way to brighten someone's day, it's a way to cope
It's a hand to hold, it's a heart to share
It's a way to spread happiness, it's a way to show you care
Kindness is a treasure, it's a gift to give
It's a way to make a difference, it's a way to live
It's a way to be a good friend, it's a way to be kind
It's a way to change the world, it's a way to shine
So let's be kind to one another, let's spread the love
Let's be there for our friends, let's rise above
Let's make the world a better place, let's make it kind
The magic of kindness, it's always on our mind.

The Beauty of Our Differences

Our differences are beautiful, they make us who we are
They're a part of our heritage, they're a shining star
Our skin is different, our hair is unique
Our culture is diverse, our history is rich
Our differences are our strength, they make us strong
They're a way to learn, they're a way to belong
Our voices are powerful, our stories are real
Our struggles and triumphs, they make us feel
Our differences are our unity, they make us one
They're a way to connect, they're a way to have fun
Our music, our dance, our art, our style
They're a way to express ourselves, they're a way to smile
So let's embrace our differences, let's celebrate
Let's be proud of who we are, let's elevate
Let's be kind to one another, let's appreciate
The beauty of our differences, let's make it great.

The Joy of Learning

Learning is a joy, it's a journey that's bright
It's a way to discover, it's a way to ignite
It's a way to explore, it's a way to grow
It's a way to challenge ourselves, it's a way to know
Learning is a gift, it's a treasure that's real
It's a way to unlock, it's a way to reveal
It's a way to inspire, it's a way to create
It's a way to imagine, it's a way to innovate
Learning is a passion, it's a love that's true
It's a way to pursue, it's a way to renew
It's a way to be curious, it's a way to be wise
It's a way to be confident, it's a way to rise
So let's embrace the joy of learning, let's open our minds
Let's be curious, let's be kind
Let's explore the world, let's find
The joy of learning, it's a treasure that's divine.

My Dreams Are Possible

My dreams are possible, they're within my reach
They're a part of me, they're what I believe
They're big and bold, they're a vision to see
My dreams are possible, they're a reality
My dreams are my inspiration, they're my motivation
They're a way to imagine, they're a way to creation
They're a way to challenge, they're a way to grow
My dreams are possible, they're a way to show
My dreams are my destiny, they're my purpose in life
They're a way to make a difference, they're a way to strive
They're a way to impact, they're a way to inspire
My dreams are possible, they're a way to aspire
So let's chase our dreams, let's make them real
Let's work hard, let's never give up, let's feel
Let's believe in ourselves, let's have faith
My dreams are possible, and that's where I'll be safe.

Legends of Our Past

In the tapestry of time, their light shines bright
Black history's heroes, warriors for what's right
They blazed trails, creating paths anew
Inspiring us all, their courage breaking through

Harriet Tubman, a beacon of hope
Leading the enslaved, helping them cope
Fearlessly she fought, never backing down
A symbol of freedom, her legacy renowned

Martin Luther King Jr., his dream held high
A voice for justice, reaching for the sky
His words ignited change, hearts were stirred
A legacy of equality, his vision still heard

Maya Angelou, her words touched the soul
With passion she wrote, making spirits whole
She taught us to rise, to find our own voice
Her wisdom and grace, forever we rejoice

Let's celebrate these legends, honor their might
Their struggles and triumphs, their guiding light
Learning from their journey, their stories inspire
Their legacy lives on, setting our hearts afire.

The Magic of Imagination

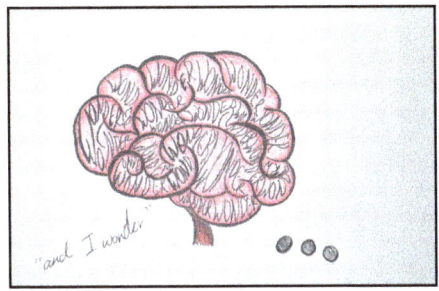

Imagination is magic, it's a world that's real
It's a way to create, it's a way to feel
It's a world of wonder, it's a world of dreams
It's a way to be free, it's a way to be seen
Imagination is power, it's a way to inspire
It's a way to imagine, it's a way to desire
It's a way to innovate, it's a way to explore
It's a way to be creative, it's a way to soar
Imagination is joy, it's a way to have fun
It's a way to play, it's a way to run
It's a way to be silly, it's a way to be wild
It's a way to be happy, it's a way to be styled
So let's embrace the magic of imagination, let's open our minds
Let's be creative, let's be kind
Let's explore our world, let's find
The magic of imagination, it's a treasure that's divine.

The Strength of Resilience

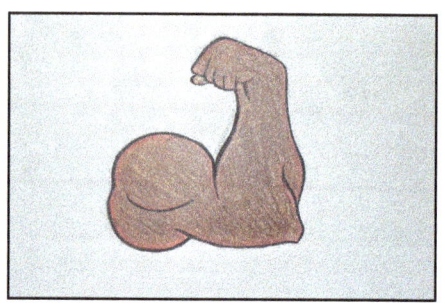

Resilience is strength, it's a way to survive
It's a way to overcome, it's a way to thrive
It's a way to face adversity, it's a way to be strong
It's a way to keep going, it's a way to belong
Resilience is courage, it's a way to be brave
It's a way to face challenges, it's a way to pave
It's a way to rise above, it's a way to grow
It's a way to be resilient, it's a way to show
Resilience is hope, it's a way to believe
It's a way to hold on, it's a way to achieve
It's a way to be positive, it's a way to be kind
It's a way to be resilient, it's a way to find
So let's embrace our resilience, let's be strong
Let's face our challenges, let's keep going, let's belong
Let's be brave, let's pave, let's grow
The strength of resilience, it's a way to show.

The Importance of Self-Love

Self-love is important, it's a way to care
It's a way to appreciate, it's a way to share
It's a way to be proud, it's a way to be true
It's a way to be happy, it's a way to be you
Self-love is acceptance, it's a way to embrace
It's a way to love our skin, it's a way to face
It's a way to be gentle, it's a way to be kind
It's a way to be patient, it's a way to unwind
Self-love is courage, it's a way to be brave
It's a way to be confident, it's a way to pave
It's a way to be strong, it's a way to be bold
It's a way to be beautiful, it's a way to be gold
As African American kids, we may face some strife
But we must love ourselves, and embrace our life
Our skin is beautiful, our hair is unique
Our culture is diverse, our history is a masterpiece
So let's embrace our self-love, let's appreciate
Let's be proud of who we are, let's elevate
Let's be kind to ourselves, let's celebrate
The importance of self-love, it's a way to be great.

About the Author

Introducing Zakara Jeña, a visionary black entrepreneur and advocate empowering African American children. With her captivating collection of poetry affirmations, Zakara Jeña combines the power of positive thinking and the joy of rhyme to inspire and uplift young minds. Her work nurtures resilience, self-assurance, and a resilient mindset, fostering confidence that will carry children through adulthood. As an entrepreneur, speaker, and advocate, Zakara Jeña champions the importance of self-belief and positivity in the lives of young black children. Join Zakara Jeña on this transformative journey of celebrating heritage and uniqueness and unlocking boundless potential. Together, let's empower the next generation on their path to greatness!

www.ingramcontent.com/pod-product-compliance
Lightning Source LLC
Chambersburg PA
CBHW060045230125
20710CB00023BA/1202